ULTRARUNNER'S
TRAINING JOURNAL,
LOG & RACING DIARY

Name: _____

Year: _____

If found, please contact me at:

_____

_____

RUNALOG°

WWW.RUNALOGS.COM

FIRST EDITION, MAY 2009.

ULTRARUNNER'S
TRAINING JOURNAL,
LOG & RACING DIARY

CONTENTS

* CUT THESE PAGES OUT AND MAKE COPIES FOR REPEAT USE

PERSONAL PROFILE

NAME: _____

ADDRESS: _____

EMAIL: _____

EMERGENCY CONTACT INFO: _____

ULTRARUNNER'S TRAINING JOURNAL

RUNALOG© **R**

compact calendar for: _____

R

MONTH				YEAR	

MONTH				YEAR	

MONTH				YEAR	

MONTH				YEAR	

MONTH				YEAR	

MONTH				YEAR	

compact calendar for: _____

R

MONTH   YEAR

MONTH   YEAR

MONTH   YEAR

MONTH   YEAR

MONTH   YEAR

MONTH   YEAR

MONTH   YEAR

MONTH   YEAR

MONTH   YEAR

MONTH   YEAR

MONTH   YEAR

MONTH   YEAR

#	race name	date	distance	time	place	notes
	_____ __ ___ _____ www:					
	_____ ___ · __ _____ www:					
	_____ ___ ___ _____ www:					
	_____ ___ ___ _____ www:					
	_____ ___ ___ _____ www:					
	_____ ___ ___ _____ www:					
	_____ ___ ___ __ _____ www:					
	_____ ___ ___ _____ www:					
	_____ ___ ___ _____ www:					
	_____ ___ ___ _____ www:					
	_____ ___ ___ _____ www:					
	_____ ___ ___ _____ www:					
	_____ ___ ___ _____ www:					
	_____ ___ ___ _____ www:					
	_____ ___ ___ _____ www:					
	_____ ___ ___ _____ www:					
	_____ ___ ___ _____ www:					
	_____ ___ ___ _____ www:					
	_____ ___ ___ _____ www:					
	_____ ___ ___ _____ www:					
	_____ ___ ___ _____ www:					
	_____ __ __ ___ _____ www:					
	_____ ___ ___ __ _____ www:					

#	race name	date	distance	time	place	notes
	www:					
	www:					
	www:					
	www:					
	www:					
	www:					
	www:					
	www:					
	www:					
	www:					
	www:					
	www:					
	www:					
	www:					
	www:					
	www:					
	www:					
	www:					
	www:					
	www:					
	www:					
	www:					
	www:					

	DISTANCES	CROSS-TRAINING	RACES	_____	MONTH'S TOTALS
JANUARY					
FEBRUARY					
MARCH					
APRIL					
MAY					
JUNE					
SUB-TOTALS					

	DISTANCES	CROSS-TRAINING	RACES	_____	MONTH'S TOTALS
JULY					
AUGUST					
SEPTEMBER					
OCTOBER					
NOVEMBER					
DECEMBER					
YEAR'S TOTALS					

ULTRARUNNER'S
TRAINING JOURNAL,
LOG & RACING DIARY

R	DATE	TIME	DISTANCE	WORKOUT CONTENT
MONDAY				
TUESDAY				
WEDNESDAY				
THURSDAY				
FRIDAY				
SATURDAY				
SUNDAY				
		TOTALS		

journal page

NOTES TO MYSELF	WEATHER	PULSE	R
		A.M.: _____ P.M.: _____	MONDAY
		A.M.: _____ P.M.: _____	TUESDAY
		A.M.: _____ P.M.: _____	WEDNESDAY
		A.M.: _____ P.M.: _____	THURSDAY
		A.M.: _____ P.M.: _____	FRIDAY
		A.M.: _____ P.M.: _____	SATURDAY
		A.M.: _____ P.M.: _____	SUNDAY

R	DATE	TIME	DISTANCE	WORKOUT CONTENT
MONDAY				
TUESDAY				
WEDNESDAY				
THURSDAY				
FRIDAY				
SATURDAY				
SUNDAY				
		TOTALS		

journal page

NOTES TO MYSELF	WEATHER	PULSE	R
		A.M.: _____ P.M.: _____	MONDAY
		A.M.: _____ P.M.: _____	TUESDAY
		A.M.: _____ P.M.: _____	WEDNESDAY
		A.M.: _____ P.M.: _____	THURSDAY
		A.M.: _____ P.M.: _____	FRIDAY
		A.M.: _____ P.M.: _____	SATURDAY
		A.M.: _____ P.M.: _____	SUNDAY

R	DATE	TIME	DISTANCE	WORKOUT CONTENT
MONDAY				
TUESDAY				
WEDNESDAY				
THURSDAY				
FRIDAY				
SATURDAY				
SUNDAY				
		TOTALS		

journal page

NOTES TO MYSELF	WEATHER	PULSE	R
		A.M.: _____ P.M.: _____	MONDAY
		A.M.: _____ P.M.: _____	TUESDAY
		A.M.: _____ P.M.: _____	WEDNESDAY
		A.M.: _____ P.M.: _____	THURSDAY
		A.M.: _____ P.M.: _____	FRIDAY
		A.M.: _____ P.M.: _____	SATURDAY
		A.M.: _____ P.M.: _____	SUNDAY

R	DATE	TIME	DISTANCE	WORKOUT CONTENT
MONDAY				
TUESDAY				
WEDNESDAY				
THURSDAY				
FRIDAY				
SATURDAY				
SUNDAY				
		TOTALS		

journal page

NOTES TO MYSELF	WEATHER	PULSE	R
		A.M.: P.M.:	MONDAY
		A.M.: P.M.:	TUESDAY
		A.M.: P.M.:	WEDNESDAY
		A.M.: P.M.:	THURSDAY
		A.M.: P.M.:	FRIDAY
		A.M.: P.M.:	SATURDAY
		A.M.: P.M.:	SUNDAY

DATES From: / / To: / /

R	DATE	TIME	DISTANCE	WORKOUT CONTENT
MONDAY				
TUESDAY				
WEDNESDAY				
THURSDAY				
FRIDAY				
SATURDAY				
SUNDAY				
		TOTALS		

journal page

NOTES TO MYSELF	WEATHER	PULSE	R
		A.M.: P.M.:	MONDAY
		A.M.: P.M.:	TUESDAY
		A.M.: P.M.:	WEDNESDAY
		A.M.: P.M.:	THURSDAY
		A.M.: P.M.:	FRIDAY
		A.M.: P.M.:	SATURDAY
		A.M.: P.M.:	SUNDAY

R	DATE	TIME	DISTANCE	WORKOUT CONTENT
MONDAY				
TUESDAY				
WEDNESDAY				
THURSDAY				
FRIDAY				
SATURDAY				
SUNDAY				
		TOTALS		

journal page

NOTES TO MYSELF	WEATHER	PULSE	R
		A.M.: P.M.:	MONDAY
		A.M.: P.M.:	TUESDAY
		A.M.: P.M.:	WEDNESDAY
		A.M.: P.M.:	THURSDAY
		A.M.: P.M.:	FRIDAY
		A.M.: P.M.:	SATURDAY
		A.M.: P.M.:	SUNDAY

R	DATE	TIME	DISTANCE	WORKOUT CONTENT
MONDAY				
TUESDAY				
WEDNESDAY				
THURSDAY				
FRIDAY				
SATURDAY				
SUNDAY				
		TOTALS		

journal page

NOTES TO MYSELF	WEATHER	PULSE	R
		A.M.: ____ P.M.: ____	MONDAY
		A.M.: ____ P.M.: ____	TUESDAY
		A.M.: ____ P.M.: ____	WEDNESDAY
		A.M.: ____ P.M.: ____	THURSDAY
		A.M.: ____ P.M.: ____	FRIDAY
		A.M.: ____ P.M.: ____	SATURDAY
		A.M.: ____ P.M.: ____	SUNDAY

R	*DATE*	*TIME*	*DISTANCE*	*WORKOUT CONTENT*
MONDAY				
TUESDAY				
WEDNESDAY				
THURSDAY				
FRIDAY				
SATURDAY				
SUNDAY				
		TOTALS		

journal page

NOTES TO MYSELF	WEATHER	PULSE	**R**
		A.M.: _____ P.M.: _____	MONDAY
		A.M.: _____ P.M.: _____	TUESDAY
		A.M.: _____ P.M.: _____	WEDNESDAY
		A.M.: _____ P.M.: _____	THURSDAY
		A.M.: _____ P.M.: _____	FRIDAY
		A.M.: _____ P.M.: _____	SATURDAY
		A.M.: _____ P.M.: _____	SUNDAY

R	DATE	TIME	DISTANCE	WORKOUT CONTENT
MONDAY				
TUESDAY				
WEDNESDAY				
THURSDAY				
FRIDAY				
SATURDAY				
SUNDAY				
		TOTALS		

NOTES TO MYSELF	WEATHER	PULSE	R
		A.M.: ___ P.M.: ___	MONDAY
		A.M.: ___ P.M.: ___	TUESDAY
		A.M.: ___ P.M.: ___	WEDNESDAY
		A.M.: ___ P.M.: ___	THURSDAY
		A.M.: ___ P.M.: ___	FRIDAY
		A.M.: ___ P.M.: ___	SATURDAY
		A.M.: ___ P.M.: ___	SUNDAY

R	DATE	TIME	DISTANCE	WORKOUT CONTENT
MONDAY				
TUESDAY				
WEDNESDAY				
THURSDAY				
FRIDAY				
SATURDAY				
SUNDAY				
		TOTALS		

NOTES TO MYSELF	WEATHER	PULSE	R
		A.M.: P.M.:	MONDAY
		A.M.: P.M.:	TUESDAY
		A.M.: P.M.:	WEDNESDAY
		A.M.: P.M.:	THURSDAY
		A.M.: P.M.:	FRIDAY
		A.M.: P.M.:	SATURDAY
		A.M.: P.M.:	SUNDAY

R	DATE	TIME	DISTANCE	WORKOUT CONTENT
MONDAY				
TUESDAY				
WEDNESDAY				
THURSDAY				
FRIDAY				
SATURDAY				
SUNDAY				
		TOTALS		

journal page

NOTES TO MYSELF	WEATHER	PULSE	R
		A.M.: _____ P.M.: _____	MONDAY
		A.M.: _____ P.M.: _____	TUESDAY
		A.M.: _____ P.M.: _____	WEDNESDAY
		A.M.: _____ P.M.: _____	THURSDAY
		A.M.: _____ P.M.: _____	FRIDAY
		A.M.: _____ P.M.: _____	SATURDAY
		A.M.: _____ P.M.: _____	SUNDAY

R	DATE	TIME	DISTANCE	WORKOUT CONTENT
MONDAY				
TUESDAY				
WEDNESDAY				
THURSDAY				
FRIDAY				
SATURDAY				
SUNDAY				
		TOTALS		

NOTES TO MYSELF	WEATHER	PULSE	R
		A.M.: _____ P.M.: _____	MONDAY
		A.M.: _____ P.M.: _____	TUESDAY
		A.M.: _____ P.M.: _____	WEDNESDAY
		A.M.: _____ P.M.: _____	THURSDAY
		A.M.: _____ P.M.: _____	FRIDAY
		A.M.: _____ P.M.: _____	SATURDAY
		A.M.: _____ P.M.: _____	SUNDAY

R	DATE	TIME	DISTANCE	WORKOUT CONTENT
MONDAY				
TUESDAY				
WEDNESDAY				
THURSDAY				
FRIDAY				
SATURDAY				
SUNDAY				
		TOTALS		

journal page

NOTES TO MYSELF	WEATHER	PULSE	**R**
		A.M.: P.M.:	MONDAY
		A.M.: P.M.:	TUESDAY
		A.M.: P.M.:	WEDNESDAY
		A.M.: P.M.:	THURSDAY
		A.M.: P.M.:	FRIDAY
		A.M.: P.M.:	SATURDAY
		A.M.: P.M.:	SUNDAY

R	DATE	TIME	DISTANCE	WORKOUT CONTENT
MONDAY				
TUESDAY				
WEDNESDAY				
THURSDAY				
FRIDAY				
SATURDAY				
SUNDAY				
	TOTALS			

journal page

NOTES TO MYSELF	WEATHER	PULSE	R
		A.M.: ___ P.M.: ___	MONDAY
		A.M.: ___ P.M.: ___	TUESDAY
		A.M.: ___ P.M.: ___	WEDNESDAY
		A.M.: ___ P.M.: ___	THURSDAY
		A.M.: ___ P.M.: ___	FRIDAY
		A.M.: ___ P.M.: ___	SATURDAY
		A.M.: ___ P.M.: ___	SUNDAY

R	DATE	TIME	DISTANCE	WORKOUT CONTENT
MONDAY				
TUESDAY				
WEDNESDAY				
THURSDAY				
FRIDAY				
SATURDAY				
SUNDAY				
		TOTALS		

journal page

NOTES TO MYSELF	WEATHER	PULSE	R
		A.M.: _____ P.M.: _____	MONDAY
		A.M.: _____ P.M.: _____	TUESDAY
		A.M.: _____ P.M.: _____	WEDNESDAY
		A.M.: _____ P.M.: _____	THURSDAY
		A.M.: _____ P.M.: _____	FRIDAY
		A.M.: _____ P.M.: _____	SATURDAY
		A.M.: _____ P.M.: _____	SUNDAY

R	DATE	TIME	DISTANCE	WORKOUT CONTENT
MONDAY				
TUESDAY				
WEDNESDAY				
THURSDAY				
FRIDAY				
SATURDAY				
SUNDAY				
		TOTALS		

journal page

NOTES TO MYSELF	WEATHER	PULSE	R
		A.M.: _____ P.M.: _____	MONDAY
		A.M.: _____ P.M.: _____	TUESDAY
		A.M.: _____ P.M.: _____	WEDNESDAY
		A.M.: _____ P.M.: _____	THURSDAY
		A.M.: _____ P.M.: _____	FRIDAY
		A.M.: _____ P.M.: _____	SATURDAY
		A.M.: _____ P.M.: _____	SUNDAY

R	DATE	TIME	DISTANCE	WORKOUT CONTENT
MONDAY				
TUESDAY				
WEDNESDAY				
THURSDAY				
FRIDAY				
SATURDAY				
SUNDAY				
		TOTALS		

journal page

NOTES TO MYSELF	WEATHER	PULSE	R
		A.M.: _____ P.M.: _____	MONDAY
		A.M.: _____ P.M.: _____	TUESDAY
		A.M.: _____ P.M.: _____	WEDNESDAY
		A.M.: _____ P.M.: _____	THURSDAY
		A.M.: _____ P.M.: _____	FRIDAY
		A.M.: _____ P.M.: _____	SATURDAY
		A.M.: _____ P.M.: _____	SUNDAY

R	DATE	TIME	DISTANCE	WORKOUT CONTENT
MONDAY				
TUESDAY				
WEDNESDAY				
THURSDAY				
FRIDAY				
SATURDAY				
SUNDAY				
		TOTALS		

journal page

NOTES TO MYSELF	WEATHER	PULSE	R
		A.M.: P.M.:	MONDAY
		A.M.: P.M.:	TUESDAY
		A.M.: P.M.:	WEDNESDAY
		A.M.: P.M.:	THURSDAY
		A.M.: P.M.:	FRIDAY
		A.M.: P.M.:	SATURDAY
		A.M.: P.M.:	SUNDAY

DATES *From:*   /   /   *To:*   /   /

R	DATE	TIME	DISTANCE	WORKOUT CONTENT
MONDAY				
TUESDAY				
WEDNESDAY				
THURSDAY				
FRIDAY				
SATURDAY				
SUNDAY				
		TOTALS		

journal page

NOTES TO MYSELF	WEATHER	PULSE	R
		A.M.: ___ ___ P.M.: ___ ___	MONDAY
		A.M.: ___ ___ P.M.: ___ ___	TUESDAY
		A.M.: ___ ___ P.M.: ___ ___	WEDNESDAY
		A.M.: ___ ___ P.M.: ___ ___	THURSDAY
		A.M.: ___ ___ P.M.: ___ ___	FRIDAY
		A.M.: ___ ___ P.M.: ___ ___	SATURDAY
		A.M.: ___ ___ P.M.: ___ ___	SUNDAY

R	DATE	TIME	DISTANCE	WORKOUT CONTENT
MONDAY				
TUESDAY				
WEDNESDAY				
THURSDAY				
FRIDAY				
SATURDAY				
SUNDAY				
		TOTALS		

NOTES TO MYSELF	WEATHER	PULSE	R
		A.M.: _____ P.M.: _____	MONDAY
		A.M.: _____ P.M.: _____	TUESDAY
		A.M.: _____ P.M.: _____	WEDNESDAY
		A.M.: _____ P.M.: _____	THURSDAY
		A.M.: _____ P.M.: _____	FRIDAY
		A.M.: _____ P.M.: _____	SATURDAY
		A.M.: _____ P.M.: _____	SUNDAY

R	DATE	TIME	DISTANCE	WORKOUT CONTENT
MONDAY				
TUESDAY				
WEDNESDAY				
THURSDAY				
FRIDAY				
SATURDAY				
SUNDAY				
		TOTALS		

journal page

NOTES TO MYSELF	WEATHER	PULSE	R
		A.M.: _____ P.M.: _____	MONDAY
		A.M.: _____ P.M.: _____	TUESDAY
		A.M.: _____ P.M.: _____	WEDNESDAY
		A.M.: _____ P.M.: _____	THURSDAY
		A.M.: _____ P.M.: _____	FRIDAY
		A.M.: _____ P.M.: _____	SATURDAY
		A.M.: _____ P.M.: _____	SUNDAY

R	DATE	TIME	DISTANCE	WORKOUT CONTENT
MONDAY				
TUESDAY				
WEDNESDAY				
THURSDAY				
FRIDAY				
SATURDAY				
SUNDAY				
	TOTALS			

journal page

NOTES TO MYSELF	WEATHER	PULSE	R
		A.M.: ____ P.M.: ____	MONDAY
		A.M.: ____ P.M.: ____	TUESDAY
		A.M.: ____ P.M.: ____	WEDNESDAY
		A.M.: ____ P.M.: ____	THURSDAY
		A.M.: ____ P.M.: ____	FRIDAY
		A.M.: ____ P.M.: ____	SATURDAY
		A.M.: ____ P.M.: ____	SUNDAY

R	DATE	TIME	DISTANCE	WORKOUT CONTENT
MONDAY				
TUESDAY				
WEDNESDAY				
THURSDAY				
FRIDAY				
SATURDAY				
SUNDAY				
		TOTALS		

journal page

NOTES TO MYSELF	WEATHER	PULSE	R
		A.M.: _____ P.M.: _____	MONDAY
		A.M.: _____ P.M.: _____	TUESDAY
		A.M.: _____ P.M.: _____	WEDNESDAY
		A.M.: _____ P.M.: _____	THURSDAY
		A.M.: _____ P.M.: _____	FRIDAY
		A.M.: _____ P.M.: _____	SATURDAY
		A.M.: _____ P.M.: _____	SUNDAY

R	DATE	TIME	DISTANCE	WORKOUT CONTENT
MONDAY				
TUESDAY				
WEDNESDAY				
THURSDAY				
FRIDAY				
SATURDAY				
SUNDAY				
		TOTALS		

NOTES TO MYSELF	WEATHER	PULSE	R
		A.M.: P.M.:	MONDAY
		A.M.: P.M.:	TUESDAY
		A.M.: P.M.:	WEDNESDAY
		A.M.: P.M.:	THURSDAY
		A.M.: P.M.:	FRIDAY
		A.M.: P.M.:	SATURDAY
		A.M.: P.M.:	SUNDAY

DATES *From:* / / *To:* / /

R	DATE	TIME	DISTANCE	WORKOUT CONTENT
MONDAY				
TUESDAY				
WEDNESDAY				
THURSDAY				
FRIDAY				
SATURDAY				
SUNDAY				
	TOTALS			

journal page

NOTES TO MYSELF	WEATHER	PULSE	R
		A.M.: _____ P.M.: _____	MONDAY
		A.M.: _____ P.M.: _____	TUESDAY
		A.M.: _____ P.M.: _____	WEDNESDAY
		A.M.: _____ P.M.: _____	THURSDAY
		A.M.: _____ P.M.: _____	FRIDAY
		A.M.: _____ P.M.: _____	SATURDAY
		A.M.: _____ P.M.: _____	SUNDAY

R	DATE	TIME	DISTANCE	WORKOUT CONTENT
MONDAY				
TUESDAY				
WEDNESDAY				
THURSDAY				
FRIDAY				
SATURDAY				
SUNDAY				
		TOTALS		

NOTES TO MYSELF	WEATHER	PULSE	R
		A.M.: _____ P.M.: _____	MONDAY
		A.M.: _____ P.M.: _____	TUESDAY
		A.M.: _____ P.M.: _____	WEDNESDAY
		A.M.: _____ P.M.: _____	THURSDAY
		A.M.: _____ P.M.: _____	FRIDAY
		A.M.: _____ P.M.: _____	SATURDAY
		A.M.: _____ P.M.: _____	SUNDAY

WEEK #: *27*   DATES From: /   /   To: /   /

R	DATE	TIME	DISTANCE	WORKOUT CONTENT
MONDAY				
TUESDAY				
WEDNESDAY				
THURSDAY				
FRIDAY				
SATURDAY				
SUNDAY				
	TOTALS			

66

NOTES TO MYSELF	WEATHER	PULSE	R
		A.M.: _____ P.M.: _____	MONDAY
		A.M.: _____ P.M.: _____	TUESDAY
		A.M.: _____ P.M.: _____	WEDNESDAY
		A.M.: _____ P.M.: _____	THURSDAY
		A.M.: _____ P.M.: _____	FRIDAY
		A.M.: _____ P.M.: _____	SATURDAY
		A.M.: _____ P.M.: _____	SUNDAY

DATES *From:* / /   *To:* / /

R	DATE	TIME	DISTANCE	WORKOUT CONTENT
MONDAY				
TUESDAY				
WEDNESDAY				
THURSDAY				
FRIDAY				
SATURDAY				
SUNDAY				
		TOTALS		

journal page

NOTES TO MYSELF	WEATHER	PULSE	R
		A.M.: _____ P.M.: _____	MONDAY
		A.M.: _____ P.M.: _____	TUESDAY
		A.M.: _____ P.M.: _____	WEDNESDAY
		A.M.: _____ P.M.: _____	THURSDAY
		A.M.: _____ P.M.: _____	FRIDAY
		A.M.: _____ P.M.: _____	SATURDAY
		A.M.: _____ P.M.: _____	SUNDAY

R	DATE	TIME	DISTANCE	WORKOUT CONTENT
MONDAY				
TUESDAY				
WEDNESDAY				
THURSDAY				
FRIDAY				
SATURDAY				
SUNDAY				
		TOTALS		

NOTES TO MYSELF	WEATHER	PULSE	R
		A.M.: P.M.:	MONDAY
		A.M.: P.M.:	TUESDAY
		A.M.: P.M.:	WEDNESDAY
		A.M.: P.M.:	THURSDAY
		A.M.: P.M.:	FRIDAY
		A.M.: P.M.:	SATURDAY
		A.M.: P.M.:	SUNDAY

DATES From: / /   To: / /

R	DATE	TIME	DISTANCE	WORKOUT CONTENT
MONDAY				
TUESDAY				
WEDNESDAY				
THURSDAY				
FRIDAY				
SATURDAY				
SUNDAY				
		TOTALS		

journal page

NOTES TO MYSELF	WEATHER	PULSE	R
		A.M.: _____ P.M.: _____	MONDAY
		A.M.: _____ P.M.: _____	TUESDAY
		A.M.: _____ P.M.: _____	WEDNESDAY
		A.M.: _____ P.M.: _____	THURSDAY
		A.M.: _____ P.M.: _____	FRIDAY
		A.M.: _____ P.M.: _____	SATURDAY
		A.M.: _____ P.M.: _____	SUNDAY

R	DATE	TIME	DISTANCE	WORKOUT CONTENT
MONDAY				
TUESDAY				
WEDNESDAY				
THURSDAY				
FRIDAY				
SATURDAY				
SUNDAY				
	TOTALS			

NOTES TO MYSELF	WEATHER	PULSE	R
		A.M.: _____ P.M.: _____	MONDAY
		A.M.: _____ P.M.: _____	TUESDAY
		A.M.: _____ P.M.: _____	WEDNESDAY
		A.M.: _____ P.M.: _____	THURSDAY
		A.M.: _____ P.M.: _____	FRIDAY
		A.M.: _____ P.M.: _____	SATURDAY
		A.M.: _____ P.M.: _____	SUNDAY

R	DATE	TIME	DISTANCE	WORKOUT CONTENT
MONDAY				
TUESDAY				
WEDNESDAY				
THURSDAY				
FRIDAY				
SATURDAY				
SUNDAY				
		TOTALS		

journal page

NOTES TO MYSELF	WEATHER	PULSE	**R**
		A.M.: ____ P.M.: ____	MONDAY
		A.M.: ____ P.M.: ____	TUESDAY
		A.M.: ____ P.M.: ____	WEDNESDAY
		A.M.: ____ P.M.: ____	THURSDAY
		A.M.: ____ P.M.: ____	FRIDAY
		A.M.: ____ P.M.: ____	SATURDAY
		A.M.: ____ P.M.: ____	SUNDAY

R	DATE	TIME	DISTANCE	WORKOUT CONTENT
MONDAY				
TUESDAY				
WEDNESDAY				
THURSDAY				
FRIDAY				
SATURDAY				
SUNDAY				
	TOTALS			

journal page

NOTES TO MYSELF	WEATHER	PULSE	R
		A.M.: _____ P.M.: _____	MONDAY
		A.M.: _____ P.M.: _____	TUESDAY
		A.M.: _____ P.M.: _____	WEDNESDAY
		A.M.: _____ P.M.: _____	THURSDAY
		A.M.: _____ P.M.: _____	FRIDAY
		A.M.: _____ P.M.: _____	SATURDAY
		A.M.: _____ P.M.: _____	SUNDAY

R	DATE	TIME	DISTANCE	WORKOUT CONTENT
MONDAY				
TUESDAY				
WEDNESDAY				
THURSDAY				
FRIDAY				
SATURDAY				
SUNDAY				
	TOTALS			

NOTES TO MYSELF	WEATHER	PULSE	R
		A.M.: P.M.:	MONDAY
		A.M.: P.M.:	TUESDAY
		A.M.: P.M.:	WEDNESDAY
		A.M.: P.M.:	THURSDAY
		A.M.: P.M.:	FRIDAY
		A.M.: P.M.:	SATURDAY
		A.M.: P.M.:	SUNDAY

R	DATE	TIME	DISTANCE	WORKOUT CONTENT
MONDAY				
TUESDAY				
WEDNESDAY				
THURSDAY				
FRIDAY				
SATURDAY				
SUNDAY				
		TOTALS		

NOTES TO MYSELF	WEATHER	PULSE	R
		A.M.: P.M.:	MONDAY
		A.M.: P.M.:	TUESDAY
		A.M.: P.M.:	WEDNESDAY
		A.M.: P.M.:	THURSDAY
		A.M.: P.M.:	FRIDAY
		A.M.: P.M.:	SATURDAY
		A.M.: P.M.:	SUNDAY

R	*DATE*	*TIME*	*DISTANCE*	*WORKOUT CONTENT*
MONDAY				
TUESDAY				
WEDNESDAY				
THURSDAY				
FRIDAY				
SATURDAY				
SUNDAY				
		TOTALS		

journal page

NOTES TO MYSELF	WEATHER	PULSE	R
		A.M.: _____ P.M.: _____	MONDAY
		A.M.: _____ P.M.: _____	TUESDAY
		A.M.: _____ P.M.: _____	WEDNESDAY
		A.M.: _____ P.M.: _____	THURSDAY
		A.M.: _____ P.M.: _____	FRIDAY
		A.M.: _____ P.M.: _____	SATURDAY
		A.M.: _____ P.M.: _____	SUNDAY

R	DATE	TIME	DISTANCE	WORKOUT CONTENT
MONDAY				
TUESDAY				
WEDNESDAY				
THURSDAY				
FRIDAY				
SATURDAY				
SUNDAY				
		TOTALS		

NOTES TO MYSELF	WEATHER	PULSE	
		A.M.: ___ P.M.: ___	MONDAY
		A.M.: ___ P.M.: ___	TUESDAY
		A.M.: ___ P.M.: ___	WEDNESDAY
		A.M.: ___ P.M.: ___	THURSDAY
		A.M.: ___ P.M.: ___	FRIDAY
		A.M.: ___ P.M.: ___	SATURDAY
		A.M.: ___ P.M.: ___	SUNDAY

R	DATE	TIME	DISTANCE	WORKOUT CONTENT
MONDAY				
TUESDAY				
WEDNESDAY				
THURSDAY				
FRIDAY				
SATURDAY				
SUNDAY				
		TOTALS		

journal page

NOTES TO MYSELF	WEATHER	PULSE	R
		A.M.: _____ P.M.: _____	MONDAY
		A.M.: _____ P.M.: _____	TUESDAY
		A.M.: _____ P.M.: _____	WEDNESDAY
		A.M.: _____ P.M.: _____	THURSDAY
		A.M.: _____ P.M.: _____	FRIDAY
		A.M.: _____ P.M.: _____	SATURDAY
		A.M.: _____ P.M.: _____	SUNDAY

DATES From: / / To: / /

R	DATE	TIME	DISTANCE	WORKOUT CONTENT
MONDAY				
TUESDAY				
WEDNESDAY				
THURSDAY				
FRIDAY				
SATURDAY				
SUNDAY				
		TOTALS		

journal page

NOTES TO MYSELF	WEATHER	PULSE	R
		A.M.: _____ P.M.: _____	MONDAY
		A.M.: _____ P.M.: _____	TUESDAY
		A.M.: _____ P.M.: _____	WEDNESDAY
		A.M.: _____ P.M.: _____	THURSDAY
		A.M.: _____ P.M.: _____	FRIDAY
		A.M.: _____ P.M.: _____	SATURDAY
		A.M.: _____ P.M.: _____	SUNDAY

R	DATE	TIME	DISTANCE	WORKOUT CONTENT
MONDAY				
TUESDAY				
WEDNESDAY				
THURSDAY				
FRIDAY				
SATURDAY				
SUNDAY				
		TOTALS		

journal page

NOTES TO MYSELF	WEATHER	PULSE	**R**
		A.M.: ⎯⎯⎯ P.M.: ⎯⎯⎯	MONDAY
		A.M.: ⎯⎯⎯ P.M.: ⎯⎯⎯	TUESDAY
		A.M.: ⎯⎯⎯ P.M.: ⎯⎯⎯	WEDNESDAY
		A.M.: ⎯⎯⎯ P.M.: ⎯⎯⎯	THURSDAY
		A.M.: ⎯⎯⎯ P.M.: ⎯⎯⎯	FRIDAY
		A.M.: ⎯⎯⎯ P.M.: ⎯⎯⎯	SATURDAY
		A.M.: ⎯⎯⎯ P.M.: ⎯⎯⎯	SUNDAY

R	DATE	TIME	DISTANCE	WORKOUT CONTENT
MONDAY				
TUESDAY				
WEDNESDAY				
THURSDAY				
FRIDAY				
SATURDAY				
SUNDAY				
		TOTALS		

journal page

NOTES TO MYSELF	WEATHER	PULSE	R
		A.M.: _____ P.M.: _____	MONDAY
		A.M.: _____ P.M.: _____	TUESDAY
		A.M.: _____ P.M.: _____	WEDNESDAY
		A.M.: _____ P.M.: _____	THURSDAY
		A.M.: _____ P.M.: _____	FRIDAY
		A.M.: _____ P.M.: _____	SATURDAY
		A.M.: _____ P.M.: _____	SUNDAY

DATES From: /   /   To: /   /

R	DATE	TIME	DISTANCE	WORKOUT CONTENT
MONDAY				
TUESDAY				
WEDNESDAY				
THURSDAY				
FRIDAY				
SATURDAY				
SUNDAY				
	TOTALS			

journal page

NOTES TO MYSELF	WEATHER	PULSE	R
		A.M.: P.M.:	MONDAY
		A.M.: P.M.:	TUESDAY
		A.M.: P.M.:	WEDNESDAY
		A.M.: P.M.:	THURSDAY
		A.M.: P.M.:	FRIDAY
		A.M.: P.M.:	SATURDAY
		A.M.: P.M.:	SUNDAY

R	DATE	TIME	DISTANCE	WORKOUT CONTENT
MONDAY				
TUESDAY				
WEDNESDAY				
THURSDAY				
FRIDAY				
SATURDAY				
SUNDAY				
		TOTALS		

journal page

NOTES TO MYSELF	WEATHER	PULSE	R
		A.M.: _____ P.M.: _____	MONDAY
		A.M.: _____ P.M.: _____	TUESDAY
		A.M.: _____ P.M.: _____	WEDNESDAY
		A.M.: _____ P.M.: _____	THURSDAY
		A.M.: _____ P.M.: _____	FRIDAY
		A.M.: _____ P.M.: _____	SATURDAY
		A.M.: _____ P.M.: _____	SUNDAY

DATES From: / /   **To:** / /

R	DATE	TIME	DISTANCE	WORKOUT CONTENT
MONDAY				
TUESDAY				
WEDNESDAY				
THURSDAY				
FRIDAY				
SATURDAY				
SUNDAY				
		TOTALS		

journal page

NOTES TO MYSELF	WEATHER	PULSE	R
		A.M.: _____ P.M.: _____	MONDAY
		A.M.: _____ P.M.: _____	TUESDAY
		A.M.: _____ P.M.: _____	WEDNESDAY
		A.M.: _____ P.M.: _____	THURSDAY
		A.M.: _____ P.M.: _____	FRIDAY
		A.M.: _____ P.M.: _____	SATURDAY
		A.M.: _____ P.M.: _____	SUNDAY

R	DATE	TIME	DISTANCE	WORKOUT CONTENT
MONDAY				
TUESDAY				
WEDNESDAY				
THURSDAY				
FRIDAY				
SATURDAY				
SUNDAY				
	TOTALS			

NOTES TO MYSELF	WEATHER	PULSE	R
		A.M.: _____ P.M.: _____	MONDAY
		A.M.: _____ P.M.: _____	TUESDAY
		A.M.: _____ P.M.: _____	WEDNESDAY
		A.M.: _____ P.M.: _____	THURSDAY
		A.M.: _____ P.M.: _____	FRIDAY
		A.M.: _____ P.M.: _____	SATURDAY
		A.M.: _____ P.M.: _____	SUNDAY

R	DATE	TIME	DISTANCE	WORKOUT CONTENT
MONDAY				
TUESDAY				
WEDNESDAY				
THURSDAY				
FRIDAY				
SATURDAY				
SUNDAY				
		TOTALS		

journal page

NOTES TO MYSELF	WEATHER	PULSE	R
		A.M.: _____ P.M.: _____	MONDAY
		A.M.: _____ P.M.: _____	TUESDAY
		A.M.: _____ P.M.: _____	WEDNESDAY
		A.M.: _____ P.M.: _____	THURSDAY
		A.M.: _____ P.M.: _____	FRIDAY
		A.M.: _____ P.M.: _____	SATURDAY
		A.M.: _____ P.M.: _____	SUNDAY

R	DATE	TIME	DISTANCE	WORKOUT CONTENT
MONDAY				
TUESDAY				
WEDNESDAY				
THURSDAY				
FRIDAY				
SATURDAY				
SUNDAY				
		TOTALS		

NOTES TO MYSELF	WEATHER	PULSE	**R**
		A.M.: _____ P.M.: _____	MONDAY
		A.M.: _____ P.M.: _____	TUESDAY
		A.M.: _____ P.M.: _____	WEDNESDAY
		A.M.: _____ P.M.: _____	THURSDAY
		A.M.: _____ P.M.: _____	FRIDAY
		A.M.: _____ P.M.: _____	SATURDAY
		A.M.: _____ P.M.: _____	SUNDAY

WEEK #: **48**   DATES From: / /   To: / /

R	DATE	TIME	DISTANCE	WORKOUT CONTENT
MONDAY				
TUESDAY				
WEDNESDAY				
THURSDAY				
FRIDAY				
SATURDAY				
SUNDAY				
		TOTALS		

journal page

NOTES TO MYSELF	WEATHER	PULSE	R
		A.M.: P.M.:	MONDAY
		A.M.: P.M.:	TUESDAY
		A.M.: P.M.:	WEDNESDAY
		A.M.: P.M.:	THURSDAY
		A.M.: P.M.:	FRIDAY
		A.M.: P.M.:	SATURDAY
		A.M.: P.M.:	SUNDAY

DATES From: / /   To: / /

R	DATE	TIME	DISTANCE	WORKOUT CONTENT
MONDAY				
TUESDAY				
WEDNESDAY				
THURSDAY				
FRIDAY				
SATURDAY				
SUNDAY				
	TOTALS			

journal page

NOTES TO MYSELF	WEATHER	PULSE	R
		A.M.: ___ P.M.: ___	MONDAY
		A.M.: ___ P.M.: ___	TUESDAY
		A.M.: ___ P.M.: ___	WEDNESDAY
		A.M.: ___ P.M.: ___	THURSDAY
		A.M.: ___ P.M.: ___	FRIDAY
		A.M.: ___ P.M.: ___	SATURDAY
		A.M.: ___ P.M.: ___	SUNDAY

R	DATE	TIME	DISTANCE	WORKOUT CONTENT
MONDAY				
TUESDAY				
WEDNESDAY				
THURSDAY				
FRIDAY				
SATURDAY				
SUNDAY				
	TOTALS			

journal page

NOTES TO MYSELF	WEATHER	PULSE	**R**
		A.M.: ____ P.M.: ____	MONDAY
		A.M.: ____ P.M.: ____	TUESDAY
		A.M.: ____ P.M.: ____	WEDNESDAY
		A.M.: ____ P.M.: ____	THURSDAY
		A.M.: ____ P.M.: ____	FRIDAY
		A.M.: ____ P.M.: ____	SATURDAY
		A.M.: ____ P.M.: ____	SUNDAY

DATES From: /   /   To: /   /

R	DATE	TIME	DISTANCE	WORKOUT CONTENT
MONDAY				
TUESDAY				
WEDNESDAY				
THURSDAY				
FRIDAY				
SATURDAY				
SUNDAY				
		TOTALS		

NOTES TO MYSELF	WEATHER	PULSE	R
		A.M.: _____ P.M.: _____	MONDAY
		A.M.: _____ P.M.: _____	TUESDAY
		A.M.: _____ P.M.: _____	WEDNESDAY
		A.M.: _____ P.M.: _____	THURSDAY
		A.M.: _____ P.M.: _____	FRIDAY
		A.M.: _____ P.M.: _____	SATURDAY
		A.M.: _____ P.M.: _____	SUNDAY

R	DATE	TIME	DISTANCE	WORKOUT CONTENT
MONDAY				
TUESDAY				
WEDNESDAY				
THURSDAY				
FRIDAY				
SATURDAY				
SUNDAY				
		TOTALS		

journal page

NOTES TO MYSELF	WEATHER	PULSE	R
		A.M.: P.M.:	MONDAY
		A.M.: P.M.:	TUESDAY
		A.M.: P.M.:	WEDNESDAY
		A.M.: P.M.:	THURSDAY
		A.M.: P.M.:	FRIDAY
		A.M.: P.M.:	SATURDAY
		A.M.: P.M.:	SUNDAY

R	DATE	TIME	DISTANCE	WORKOUT CONTENT
MONDAY				
TUESDAY				
WEDNESDAY				
THURSDAY				
FRIDAY				
SATURDAY				
SUNDAY				
	TOTALS			

journal page

NOTES TO MYSELF	WEATHER	PULSE	R
		A.M.: ____ P.M.: ____	MONDAY
		A.M.: ____ P.M.: ____	TUESDAY
		A.M.: ____ P.M.: ____	WEDNESDAY
		A.M.: ____ P.M.: ____	THURSDAY
		A.M.: ____ P.M.: ____	FRIDAY
		A.M.: ____ P.M.: ____	SATURDAY
		A.M.: ____ P.M.: ____	SUNDAY

ULTRARUNNER'S
TRAINING JOURNAL,
LOG & RACING DIARY

APPENDIX PAGES:

CUT THESE OUT AND MAKE
MULTIPLE COPIES FOR FUTURE USE

shopping list

item	group	est. cost	final cost	totals	√

item	group	est. cost	final cost	totals	√

my today's running route

Today's date: _____

training location:	I am leaving at: (TIME) _____	should be back at: (TIME) _____

drawing of the map of my training's location, or the route's description:

N

W   E

S

if not back by: _____ (time), call: _____

RUNALOG® **R**   *my today's running route*

Today's date: _____

training location:	I am leaving at:	should be back at:
_____	(TIME) _____	(TIME)_____

drawing of the map of my training's location, or the route's description:

if not back by:_____(time), call: _____

my favorite running routes

#	Route's Name/Location	Distance	Terrain	Notes

 RUNALOG® R

my favorite running routes

#	Route's Name/Location	Distance	Terrain	Notes

contacts

NAME	ADDRESS	PHONE/CELL	EMAIL

NAME	ADDRESS	PHONE/CELL	EMAIL

racing diary

date	race name	time	place

date	race name	time	place

racing diary

date	race name	time	place

date	race name	time	place

date	race name	time	place

date	race name	time	place

date	race name	time	place

date	race name	time	place

racing diary

date	race name	time	place

date	race name	time	place

date	race name	time	place

date	race name	time	place

date	race name	time	place

date	race name	time	place

date	race name	time	place

date	race name	time	place

racing diary

date	race name	time	place

date	race name	time	place

date	race name	time	place

date	race name	time	place

date	race name	time	place

date	race name	time	place

date	race name	time	place

date	race name	time	place

racing diary

date	race name	time	place

date	race name	time	place

date	race name	time	place

date	race name	time	place

racing diary

date	race name	time	place

date	race name	time	place

racing diary

date	race name	time	place

date	race name	time	place

racing diary

date	race name	time	place

date	race name	time	place

date	race name	time	place

date	race name	time	place

date	race name	time	place

date	race name	time	place

date	race name	time	place

date	race name	time	place

Made in the USA